The
Ultimate
Choice

Determines Our Destiny

By Tony Zeiss

Published by
Spiritbuilding Publishers
9700 Ferry Road, Waynesville, Ohio 45068

THE ULTIMATE CHOICE
Determines Our Destiny
By Tony Zeiss

ISBN: 978–1–964–80526–9

Spiritbuilding
PUBLISHERS

spiritbuilding.com

Table of Contents

Preface 1

Introduction 4

Chapter 1   Life's Essential Questions 9

Chapter 2   Biblical Answers to Life's Questions I 16

Chapter 3   Biblical Answers to Life's Questions II 26

Chapter 4   God's Universal Law 43

Chapter 5   A Quick Look at His Universe 54

Chapter 6   Our Reasonable Service 61

Chapter 7   Seek Wisdom Not Gold 66

References 71

Preface

Greetings! You are about to read this Bible-based primer that can equip you with the knowledge to achieve things beyond your dreams today and for eternity! I congratulate you and encourage you to embrace this narrative based on our Creator's words. Strap on your seat belt, it will be a supernatural, thrilling, and eye-opening experience.

The purpose of this small volume is to introduce and reinforce God's plan for your life. Time spent with this book will inspire some serious reflection about your current circumstances. Life on Earth is often confusing and disappointing, but there are Godly principles that will provide clarity and joy. You will be given some astonishing options to ensure that your future is also meaningful and gratifying.

This primer is not intended to judge or force anything on anyone. It does recognize the truth that all of us sin and fall short of the glory of the Lord, but God gives us opportunities to be forgiven and lead meaningful and exciting lives by making good choices.

Making good choices is not an accident. We cannot depend on our instincts or our fleshly desires to lead us to happiness. We have to turn to God's truth through His word to equip ourselves to make good choices that produce happiness. We have to intentionally determine how to consistently make good, productive decisions.

There are many people who have never heard about our Creator or His plan for our salvation and living purposeful lives here and hereafter.

For example, some people live in remote areas and speak unique languages and don't have missionaries or even Bibles in their language. The Wycliffe Global Alliance estimates there are about 7,000 languages in the world and 985 of them have no Bibles translated in their language. Thousands of others only have partial translations. Even in countries that have Bibles, many people do not yet recognize the amazing things God wants them to accept to improve their lives.

Our Creator wishes that all of us would make the choice to accept his Son as our Savior and lead servant-focused lives. Therefore, this discourse emphasizes the subject of personal happiness and improvement to all who read this narrative. I am especially focused on teenagers and young adults because they are at the age when most of us wrestle with the great questions of life. The world does not have the answers to life's essential questions; God has those answers and we will review them in Chapters One and Two.

There are two major options for living: 1. We choose to live for ourselves, and pursue worldly things, or 2. We choose to live for Christ and serve His cause. The aim of this primer is to:

Help people discover, restore, or reinforce their walk with the Lord.

It is my hope that each of you will gain a greater understanding and love for God, His Son Jesus, and the Holy Spirit as you face or reface the critical choices in your life.

If you haven't determined who you will serve in this life, this book will put it in perspective so you can make an informed decision.

If you formerly made a decision to follow Jesus, but have drifted away for some reason, the information you are about to read will help you recall the blessings of living with Christ rather than without Him.

If you are a committed Christian, this narrative will be very helpful in reinforcing your walk with Christ and making you better prepared to deal with life's struggles. It will also be a stimulating source of information that will increase your confidence as you tell others about your Christian experience.

There are many lengthy books written on this topic. Hopefully this brief digest enlightens your Biblical knowledge, gives you a healthy appetite to learn more from the Bible and proves to be useful to you in this very busy world. It is my hope that you will actively pursue and engage in a life with Jesus. It will be the best decision of your life.

I am a life-long Christian, but I am not an academic theologian. I have been a dedicated educator, author, speaker, historian, and a husband, father, and grandfather. I have been blessed with a Christ-confident wife and good family. God gave me the opportunity to be a church leader and Bible teacher for decades, and I was honored to be recruited by the David Green family to become the first Executive Director of Museum of the Bible in Washington, D. C. This primer is the work of a grateful person who wishes to assist others in their walk through this life and the next one.

Like all Christians, I strive to be worthy of that name. It has been an exciting journey of learning and maturing in my mind, heart, and soul. We are the only living beings to whom God gave an eternal soul. It is an incredible gift for sure. It is my intent that this book will be a soul-affirming expedition for you.

My friend and well known South Carolina preacher, Jeff Trotter, once gave a sermon on this topic explaining, "The fundamental question is not what God wants us to do, but what God want us to be." This is an insightful statement and one we will examine throughout the book.

Introduction

We Christians are not saved so we can relax for the rest of our lives on this Earth. The Christian experience is far more exciting than that. Once we surrender ourselves to Jesus, our Savior, life gets more exciting and rewarding than we ever imagined. A retired preacher and friend, Jim Mullican says, "Nothing worthwhile ever happens by accident and you can't drift upstream. Life takes work!" When we are working for the Lord, it is demanding, sometimes intimidating, but always rewarding. Over time, we realize that things happen according to God's plan, not ours, and we begin to recognize that we learn best from our failures. We also discern that kindness and goodness are their own rewards as suggested in Proverbs 11:17–19. In addition, a servant-oriented life provides amazing meaning to our lives and pleases God, our Creator.

Some people have the mistaken idea that life is boring for Christians because they can't enjoy the fun things of the world. Actually, it is just the opposite. Christians are having the best time of their lives working with the Holy Trinity to grow in the knowledge and faith of God and to help lead others to the church kingdom that Jesus established. The word Trinity describes the Godhead that includes God, Jesus, and the Holy Spirit. Christians' lives are enriched with God's truth, love, and mercy. The Bible also equips us with the knowledge, wisdom, faith, and prayer skills necessary to serve with Jesus, the Holy Spirit, and God in many meaningful, rewarding, and beneficial ways.

God's Biblical Revelations explain that all humans understand His invisible qualities and will seek Him as told in Romans 1:20 and Jeremiah 29:13. Most people feel an inherited Godly urge to serve others in need as evidenced in every catastrophic circumstance that affects people.

Hurricane Helene swept through western North Carolina in the fall of 2024 and was no exception. Before the rain stopped, neighbors were outside with chainsaws cutting fallen trees out of roads and driveways to help our communities. Within two days, churches and other religious organizations were collecting and distributing clothing, food, and generators to storm victims. A few weeks later, charitable and religious groups began building custom bridges over streams so people could access their homes. Other groups built small houses for people who lost their homes. People all over America willingly pitched in to help others. Those compassionate people were honoring God and His Son with their selfless work. We seem to have Godly compassion for others built into our DNA.

God's greatest gift to us is our Lord and Savior, Jesus the Christ. The best way to learn about Jesus is to read the scriptures of the Bible. They are illuminating, comforting, and informative. The Bible provides hope for the hopeless, strength for the weak, assurance for those who doubt, victory in Christ, life in abundance, the path to righteousness, spiritual guidance, and personal growth.

This Bible is the most incredible book ever written and is the best-selling book of all time. It is the foundation for no less than seven major religions and it is the most controversial and debated book of all ages. Yet, to believers, it is unquestionably the Living Word of God, the grand architect of our universe.

I once had a friend ask me what my favorite book of all time was. "The Bible," I replied. "I meant a real book," he blurted. "The Bible is a real Book."

Let me assure you there is no other book that comes close to the significance of this Godly gift. In *Evidence That Demands a Verdict,* by Josh and Sean McDowell, we read, "Clearly, the Bible has influenced civilization more than any other literary work in history." (13) In the concluding remarks about *Museum of the Bible*, it reads, "The Bible is a central piece of humanity's shared history ... worthy of continued investigation, critical engagement, and appreciation." (20)

The Bible has survived two thousand years of Satan-induced criticism, but God's truth prevails. This amazing book includes the Old Testament, which was God's covenant with the Hebrew people, and the New Testament, which is the new covenant under which people of all nations live today. God spoke to the Hebrews through His prophets during the Old Testament and spoke to all people through Jesus in the New Testament. Both sections of the Bible are profitable for learning God's truth and His will for us. Those who accept Jesus as their savior are commonly referred to as Christians and they follow the teachings of Jesus in the New Testament.

Today, there are about 2.4 billion Christians, the largest religious group in the world, who depend upon this book as the basis for their faith and the way they live their lives.

Here is a little known fact we should all remember: God's Word is *"active and alive."* (Hebrews 4:12) As we read and hear it, we begin to incorporate His ways into our lives. In the book of Isaiah 55:11 God says, *"So shall My Word be which goes forth from my mouth; It shall not return to Me empty, without accomplishing what I desire, and without succeeding in the matter for which I sent it."* His Word is true in all that He says and so are His promises. For example, he says there is power in prayer and all Christians will testify to this truth.

As a personal example, in the summer of 2016, I announced my retirement from Central Piedmont Community College in Charlotte, North Carolina, after 24 years as President. Soon thereafter, on a Saturday, I prayed with my wife Beth for God to let us know what He wanted us to do next since we would soon have some time on our hands. On Monday afternoon, I received a call from the owner of a California search firm. He said that he represented an international Bible organization that was planning to build the first comprehensive Museum of the Bible in the world. He explained that it would be located in Washington D. C. near the national capital and they wanted me to be the founding Executive Director of that project. I immediately remembered my prayer. The prayers of Christians are powerful because they are heard by God, (John 9:31).

Four months later, we moved to Washington, D. C. to take on one of the most wonderful and challenging projects in our lives. This example is only one of millions of similar examples of how God plans and directs our paths once we commit to Him, His Son, and the Holy Spirit.

I am excited and honored that you are reading this narrative. Chapter one deals with life's essential questions. It took me about seven decades to learn how to fully answer the questions that lead us through life. You will get them much faster than that!

It is my prayer that each reader of this primer will have a receptive mind, heart, and soul. You can expect to be stimulated, informed, and edified.

This is your journey, your search for meaningfulness, and your opportunity to confidently take charge of the choices that determine your destiny.

Notes: Jesus holds the Godly title of the Greek word *Christós* or Christ which means "The Anointed One", Savior of the World. Biblical scripture often refers to Jesus and (the) Christ as the same person, which is correct. Jesus is also referred to as Lord, Savior, Immanuel (God with us), the Lamb of God (Jesus's holy sacrifice on the cross) and a host of other positive descriptors.

To keep this primer limited in narrative, I will cite samples of scripture as appropriate to emphasize and verify main points in the text. Each topic cited by scripture will likely have additional verses on the same topic in the Bible. All printed scripture will be italicized and I will paraphrase others, but cite the verses.

The Biblical scripture cited in this work comes from *The New American Standard Bible* except where otherwise noted. The (KJV) represents the King James Version and the (NIV) represents the *New International Version*.

Get ready for an Illuminating experience into life's critical questions; God's Word; His son, Jesus; His universe and its major law; the Holy Spirit; and God's wisdom. We will begin by addressing some of life's most important questions.

Chapter 1
Life's Essential Questions

As we mature in life, most of us begin to ask ourselves some pertinent questions about our existence and how we fit into the world. These key questions eventually demand some important personal conclusions and choices that influence the direction of our lives on this Earth and beyond. Some of those questions most often talked about with family, friends, and clergy include:

1. Is God real?
2. What is my purpose in life?
3. Who created the universe?
4. Why was I created?
5. How do I find truth to guide my life?
6. What should I do about Jesus?
7. What must I do to be saved?
8. What kind spouse and career should I seek?

Hopefully, you have already pondered these and other questions as you seek to navigate through this life of wonders, love, hope, and faith. Of course, we also must work through the opposite human experiences including apprehension, hate, despair, and emptiness. In this world of opposites, it is necessary that we learn to make good choices rather than bad choices regarding this extraordinary thing we call life.

Here are some additional common worldly opposites:

1. Will you live this life you have been given as a good person or bad person?

2. Will you choose to seek righteousness or wickedness?
3. How can you determine what is good or bad, righteous or evil, truth or lies?

These are healthy questions because God has given all of us the precious gift of life, and with it, the free will to choose what kind of life we wish to live. My purpose in writing this chapter is to equip you with the knowledge of how to make excellent earthly and heavenly choices as you live temporarily in this world and anticipate living permanently in heaven. As we consider these questions, we should be aware of the truth in Proverbs 21:2, *"Every man's way is right in his own eyes, but the Lord weighs the hearts."* God looks at the motives behind our thoughts and actions.

We live in a complex world. Psychologists, philosophers, scientists, and millions of confused people wrestle with these questions unless they know where to go for trustworthy answers. For them, it is like trying to drive across the country without GPS or a road map. Our best opportunity to discover the right answer is to seek truth as our guide. The only real truth in this world and the next is in God's Word, where we should look for answers to all our questions. We Christians use the Bible as our lifelong GPS to navigate through this life.

A little further in this narrative, we will see that clarity does evolve from confusion and order does come from chaos, if we follow God's truth and understand His rules. If not, we deceive ourselves. In Bible history, we learn that God gives all of us a choice to live a life with unforgiven transgressions, tribulation, and confusion or we can live a life with His son, Jesus, who grants total forgiveness, order, and peace.

Now let's first look at some practical things about your life. God has a positive plan for your life, found in Jeremiah 29:11. In Proverbs 16:9 we are told, *"The mind of man plans his way, but the Lord directs his steps."* However, we must allow the Lord to direct our steps. Life is full of choices. We can choose to live with or without His direction. All of us have a choice to determine whether we wish to become affirmed by our Creator or not.

If we choose a self-centered lifestyle, we most likely are seeking the approval of other people. We all do this to some degree because it is part of our nature. But if that approval becomes the driving force of our lives, we have become slaves to a false God that can never be satisfied. John Ortberg, a preacher and author of the book, "The Life You've Always Wanted" warns that, "Approval addicts find themselves measuring their accomplishments against those of other people." (160) This chasing your tail exercise produces a lifetime of frustration.

Another possible course is to pursue the worldly pleasures of lust, fame, power, and fortune. These do not produce meaningfulness, happiness, or contentment. However, a life that is being transformed into the spiritual joys of the Lord does produce these lasting benefits.

Purposeful and satisfying lives evolve from knowing and pleasing God with the blessings He provides through His Son. We will assume that you are thinking that a Godly life will be your best pursuit, rather than a life of egotistical and carnal pursuits that will have no glory in the end.

James Allen, the acclaimed British author of, *As A Man Thinketh*, inspired by Proverbs 23:7, wrote this applicable advice:

> Man is made or unmade by himself; in the armory of thought he forges the weapons by which he destroys himself, he also fashions the tools with which he builds for himself heavenly mansions of joy and strength and peace. By the right choice and true application of thought, man ascends to the divine perfection; by the abuse and wrong application of thought, he descends below the level of the beast.

Books about the mind and its power are fascinating, but we must remember that our minds and our very existence come from God Almighty and His Word. God is the universal mind behind everything ever created or thought about.

The astonishing thing about God's gift of life is our ability to think for ourselves. Our thoughts are things in themselves. They influence our decisions and our actions. Those thoughts we dwell on tend to manifest themselves whether they are good or evil in the eyes of God. We must learn to govern our thoughts in order to govern ourselves. We truly become what we choose to think about. Wise people learn to control their thoughts.

Faith and Belief

In Matthew 9:28 we learn that Jesus is talking to some blind men who came to Him for help. In Matthew 9:29 we are told, *"Then He touched their eyes, saying, 'Be it done to you according to your faith.'"* In many other examples of healing in the New Testament, Jesus relates the healing to the person's faith or belief. Belief and faith are often interchangeable, as in this situation. This is a key to success for what we ask in prayer. For example, in Matthew 21:22 Jesus tells His disciples, *"And all things you ask in prayer believing, you shall receive."*

Each of us who aspire to live productive and gratifying lives must learn to discern what we choose to think about and believe. However, faith is actually a stronger spiritual emotion than belief, in that it requires more trust. Faith is defined in Paul's letter to the Hebrews 11:1, *"Now faith is the assurance of things hoped for, the conviction of things not seen."*

The famous German theologian, Dietrich Bonhoeffer, wrote a detailed letter to his unbelieving brother-in-law, Rudiger Schleicher in 1936 encouraging him to read the Bible about the saving grace of Jesus and the transforming power of God's Word. Bonhoeffer was saddened to receive Schleicher's return letter saying all he saw in the Bible were words, nothing inspiring. Bonhoeffer responded, "Only if we expect from it the ultimate answer, shall we receive it." (Newstimes.org, December 2024) Good advice from a faithful man who gave his life to Christ. Here is what God had to say about faith in Jeremiah 29:13 as Jeremiah the prophet spoke to the Jewish leaders in captivity at Babylonia, *"And you will seek Me and find Me when you search for Me with all your heart."* Luke, the author of Acts, says God knows about our hearts, (Acts 15:8). Two verses later, in Acts, 15:9, Jesus makes no distinction between Jews and Gentiles and said He cleanses their hearts by faith.

The art of self-discipline is best accomplished by immersing ourselves in God's righteousness and by learning and trusting His truth. Incredibly, He tells us what we should be thinking about, Philippians 4:8 says, *"Finally, brethren, whatever is true, whatever is honorable, whatever is right, whatever is pure, whatever is lovely, whatever is of good repute, if there is any excellence and if anything worthy of praise, let your mind dwell on these things."*

But God does even more than that, He gives us a prescription for living a valuable and blessed life in Philippians 4:4–7, *"Rejoice in the Lord always, again I will say, rejoice! Be anxious for nothing, but in everything by prayer and supplication with thanksgiving let your requests be made known to God. And the peace of God, which surpasses all comprehension, shall guard your hearts and your minds in Christ Jesus."* This Godly prescription for living a blessed life is perfect advice for those who lived before us, those of us today, and those in the future. This verse should be taped on the bathroom mirror or the refrigerator to remind us how to live.

Hearts

The Bible also warns us about what we should avoid thinking about as provided in the Psalms, Proverbs, and throughout the New Testament. God repeatedly states that the righteous are tested, but He hates the wicked. The wicked produce evil while the righteous produce good fruit of the spirit including love, joy, and kindness. The Apostle Paul gives us a stark contrast of the behavior of wicked people and righteous people in Ephesians 4:31–32, *"Let all bitterness and wrath and anger and clamor and slander be put away from you, along with all malice. And be kind to one another, tender hearted, forgiving each other, just as God in Christ also has forgiven you."* This verse also qualifies to be put on the mirror or the refrigerator.

In a popular bible research book, *Evidence That Demands A Verdict,* we are told that the Bible has many verses that concern our minds and what we think, but there are five times as many verses about our hearts. (703) The authors conclude that God is interested in communicating with us on a heart-to-heart basis, as well as an intellectual basis. Our hearts help manifest our beliefs, desires, and faith. If our beliefs, desires, and faith are in God and His plans for us, our hearts will favor those virtues. However, if our beliefs, desires, and faith are about ourselves and worldly accomplishments, our hearts will favor the advancement of those temporary and worldly pursuits. We should be focusing on achieving things in God's will, not out own. Matthew 6:21 explains it clearly, *"For where your treasure is, there will your heart be also."* God knows our hearts, (Luke 16:15).

The world is full of well-meaning, but unreliable statements about the heart like: "Just trust your heart, and everything will work out for the best." Our hearts are not all-knowing, benevolent guides for our lives. They are not righteous by nature. Jeremiah 17:9 tells us that the heart is most deceitful and none can understand it. Numbers 15:39–40 warned the Jewish people to follow the commands of the Lord and not their own hearts. Matthew 15:18–19 tells us that evil things come from our hearts including vile thoughts, murders, adulteries, fornications, thefts, false witness and the like.

The heart promotes evil, but also emanates compassion and is place of love. In this respect, Proverbs 4:23 advises, *"Trust in the Lord with all your heart, and do not lean on your own understanding."* The prophet Jeremiah was right to ask, *"Who can understand it?"* (Jeremiah 17:9). The best thing we can do when considering choices is to use our minds objectively, without any ungodly emotions or desires to influence us.

The Bible

God's remarkable Bible was written by about forty men over a span of about 1,400 years. These blessed men came from all walks of life, educational attainment, and backgrounds. It was written in three languages, Hebrew, Greek, and Aramaic. It is astounding that this Word of God does not contradict itself even though so many people from diverse backgrounds and knowledge wrote it over so many years. However, we can be assured that all these Biblical authors were divinely inspired as we are told in 2 Timothy 3:16–17: *"All scripture is inspired by*

God and profitable for teaching, for reproof, for correction, for training in righteousness; that the man of God may be adequate, equipped for every good work."

We are blessed to have God's truth and His Word, to guide us as we make choices. The more we absorb His words into our minds and hearts, the easier it becomes to make good choices. Over time we either know how God feels about a situation or we learn to check what His word says before taking any action. Important decisions should be made from His wisdom before we exhaust ourselves trying to make the decision without God's advice. Praying for assistance and searching His Word in the first place makes our choices infinitely easier.

In these prayers we should ask for God's help for us to understand and make right choices. Reviewing His Word concerning your decisions will astound you. There are some Bible-based internet sites that can be very helpful in finding what scripture says about almost anything on your mind, but be discerning because some sites are actually pushing ideas opposed to or not in Biblical scripture.

In the meantime, grab a tight rein like your life depends upon it. The second chapter is full of supernatural information as we consider Biblical answers to life's common questions!

Chapter 2

Biblical Answers to Life's Questions I

Let's look at the first five life-directing questions.

#1
Is God real?

This is an important question that all of us must determine for ourselves. The best source for this answer is, of course, the Bible. Its books were confirmed by at least three groups of early Christian scholars. These dedicated Christian leaders included the Council of Nicaea in 325, the Council of Hippo in 393, and the Councils of Carthage in 337 and 419. History documents that thousands of Christians were martyred for the sake of their allegiance to God and His Son when Jewish and Roman leaders banned this new following. Eleven of the first twelve Disciples of Christ gave up their lives for Jesus and His desire to establish His Kingdom (church) on Earth. John, the youngest disciple, spent most of his last years incarcerated in a cave on the Island of Patmos in the Aegean Sea.

Steve Green, the founder of Museum of the Bible and his cowriter, Todd Hillard, quoted what the historically famous scientist Sir Isaac Newton said about God in their 2013 book, *The Bible in America*. Newton said, "Gravity explains the motions of the planets, but it cannot explain who set the planets in motion. God governs all things and knows all that is or can be done."(53) These authors also made this observation: Today, the Bible is present in nearly every home and accessible to all in multiple formats online. The vast majority of Americans believe that it is the true, inspired Word of God. Mounting manuscript evidence and archaeological discoveries continue to affirm its authority and accuracy. We can now prove that Scripture engagement is a vital key for spiritual growth. (141)

Historical and archaeological records give evidence of the truth of the Bible. Christianity, as we know, is the largest religion in the world. In the acclaimed book, *Fulfilled Prophecy: Evidence for the Reliability of the Bible,* author Hugh Ross shares some of his book's research on the accuracy of Biblical prophecies in an online article for Reasons to Believe. "Unique among all books ever written, the Bible accurately foretells specific events in detail many years, sometimes centuries, before they occur. Approximately 2,500 prophecies appear in the pages of the Bible. About 2,000 of which have already been fulfilled to the letter, no errors." Ross also explains that the remaining 500 reach into the future and the possibility of the first 2,000 prophesies happening by chance is less than one in ten, with 2000 zeros!"

Aside from these and other research reports about the accuracy and reliability of the truth of the Bible, I believe the Bible itself best attests to its accuracy and reliability.

In Matthew 7:7, Jesus told the Hebrew people in His day to *"Ask and it will be given to you; seek and you will find; knock and the door will be opened to you."* In Hebrews 4:12 we already learned that the word is *"active and alive."* These promises are true and dependable and millions of past and present Christians have testified to this fact. Granted, we may not always get what we pray for in the time we want it, but if our request is in concert with God's will, it will be granted in His chosen time. When we Christians don't receive the answer we hope for, we are comforted by His promise in Romans 8:28, *"And we know that God causes all things to work together for good to those who love God, to those who are called according to His purpose."*

As we hear, read, and study God's Word, its truth and His kingdom are evident. God bears witness to Himself with every word in the Bible, bird in the air, and fish in the sea. Evidence of God is everywhere. Psalms 19:1 is one of my favorite verses and illustrates His omnipresence. The New International Bible (NIV) reads, *"The heavens declare the glory of God; the skies proclaim the work of His hands."* He is also evident in every kindness including His Son, the Savior whom he freely gives us when we choose to follow Him. Another favorite verse of mine in Ephesians 2:8 illustrates that God even gives us the faith we need to accept Jesus as our Savior. *"For by grace you have been saved through faith; and that not of yourselves, it is the gift of God."*

Moses was inspired by the Holy Spirit to begin Genesis 1:1, *"In the beginning God created the Heavens and the Earth."* Our very existence and the entire universe are evidence that God is real.

#2
What Is My Purpose in Life?

The Bible has many verses in the Old and New Testaments that help us understand our purpose. Rick Warren, a world-renowned preacher and friend, wrote a best-selling book on this topic, "The Purpose Driven Life." His first sentence in the book summarizes the most important thing we must realize as we consider what to do with our lives. "It's not about you." We humans are egocentric by nature, but as we read the Bible, it is clear that God wants us to surrender ourselves to His love, protection, and commandments.

Matthew 22:36–39 provides the first two great commandments to *"Love God"* and *"Love our neighbors as ourselves."* God's great commission for all Christians is found in Matthew 28:19–20: *"Go therefore and make disciples of all the nations, baptizing them in the name of the Father, and the Son, and the Holy Spirit. Teaching them to observe all that I commanded you."* During the Roman Imperial period, Seneca, the revered Stoic philosopher, stated that "might makes right." Centuries later, President

Lincoln declared that "right makes might." Ole Abe was correct: God's Words, truth, and righteousness beat man's words and speculation every time. As recorded in Matthew 5:10, *"Blessed are those who have been persecuted for the sake of righteousness, for theirs is the kingdom of heaven."*

In summary, our Godly purpose is to:

1. Love God with all our heart, soul, and mind, Matthew 22:36–40.
2. Accept Jesus and the Holy Spirit through baptism, Acts 2:38; Colossians 2:12.
3. Follow God's commandments, Matthew 22:37–38.
4. Spread the Gospel, Matthew 28:19–20; Do good works, Ephesians 2:10;
5. Walk in a worthy manner, Ephesians 4:1–6;
6. Be instruments of righteousness, Romans 6:13;
7. Be kind to one another, Ephesians 4:31–32.
8. Overcome evil with good, Romans 12:21. (might makes right)

#3
Who Created the Universe?

Unfortunately, there are still people who believe humans evolved from lesser life forms all the way back to the single-celled Amoeba. This thinking was spawned when Charles Darwin published his popular book, "On the Origin of Species," in 1859. Soon thereafter, many uninformed science teachers began teaching evolution instead of creationism. The 1925 Scopes trial (debate) in Kentucky, ushered in evolution to replace creationism in our public schools. In the Bible, God warns us repeatedly about Satan's deceptions through human action. Psalm 118:8, the middle verse of the Bible, tells us: *"It is better to take refuge in the Lord than to trust in man."* Satan deceives humans to do his work on Earth.

Of course, Satan is still hard at work trying to keep people from serving God and living eternally with Him. The great deceiver was the one who convinced Judas Iscariot to betray Jesus, (John 13:27). This "father of lies" continues to deceive people today. Every time we hear about people who have committed evil deeds, we witness Satan at work.

The teaching of evolution is still dominating our science classes in public schools today, yet there is no mention in the Bible that any species would or could evolve into a different species. It is not surprising that scientists have not found any evidence of evolution. Even if scientists could prove some example of evolution, it would still beg the question of who or how the first life forms were created. Evolutionists cannot explain away intelligent design by God.

Proving evolution is not the primary motivator of people who promote it to our children. Their primary motivation is to teach new generations that God does not exist and man knows best how to lead the masses. It is a colossal satanic deception that tries to pit man's science against Gods Word.

In truth, science and creationism are mostly in harmony as advanced science slowly catches up with Biblical truths. For example, biblical scripture from 3,500 years ago describes how water moves from oceans, lakes, and streams from one part of the Earth to another in the form of clouds and rain to sustain plant and animal life. (Job 26:18)

As we have already learned, Genesis 1:27 (KJV) clearly articulates that God almighty created us: *"And God created man in his own image, in the image of God he created him; Male and Female, He created them."* Colossians 1:16–17 explains that Jesus was instrumental in creation, *"For by Him (Jesus) all things were created, both in heaven and on earth, visible and invisible … And He is before all things, and in Him all things hold together."* I think of God as the grand architect and Jesus as the construction manager of the universe. Of course, the Holy Spirit was also present during creation, (Genesis 1:2).

#4
Why Was I Created?

Each person was created by God and given free will to become whatever his or her heart and mind lead them to be. However, God wishes for us to live righteously and glorify Him. (John 15:8) This free will is not God's permission to do evil or immoral things. God provides clear moral choices for us in His word. We have an obligation to read about His righteous expectations.

To fully discover His expectations and answer this question, we must turn to the Bible. From studying it, we learn that we have to decide whether we will follow Jesus or wing it on our own. There are only two choices with this question: we chose to follow Jesus or reject Him. As recorded in John 14:6, Jesus told Thomas, His disciple, *"I am the way, and the truth, and the life; no one comes to the Father, but through me.* Genesis 1:26–27 describes all humans as creations of God, made in His image. The Bible also says we, who are in Christ, are children of God, (Galatians 3:26).

If we want answers to life's big questions and if we want security, happiness, and life everlasting, there is only one way to get it. We can't buy it or earn it. Accepting the grace of God faithfully through baptism and serving Jesus, the Redeemer of our sins, is the only way these things can be permanently acquired. Ephesians 2:10 tells us, *"For we are His workmanship, created in Christ Jesus for good works, which God prepared beforehand, that we should walk in them."*

By hearing and reading His scripture, we can clearly see that yielding to God's will for us to accept His Son as our Savior and be baptized is the only good answer to this critical question. God wants us to choose to become Christians, His children, and members of His kingdom here and forever, (1 Peter 1:3, 4).

God placed humans above every other living species, even above the Angels. Genesis 1:28 states that humans are superior to all other animal species and should rule over every living thing that moves on the Earth. In 1 Corinthians 6:3 Paul says; *"Do you not know that we shall judge Angels...?"*

God sees Christians as becoming extensions of His Kingdom and glory serving the cause of Christ who came to seek and save the lost, (Luke 19:10).

God created us for His glory. (Matthew 5:16) And He commanded us to love Him with all our heart, soul, and mind as we have already seen, (Matthew 22:37).

Adam and Eve, the first humans on earth made a terrible choice by disobeying God, and sin filled the earth through the work of Satan and bad choices by humans. God prepared His Son Jesus to sacrifice himself as the Savior of all people who believe and accept Him. Those who do this will receive the Holy Spirit and become members of His kingdom on Earth and in Heaven. We are God's children and the main object of His will and His universe. The major steps of God's plan are:

1. God created us and loves us.
2. All people are in a fallen world and are sinful.
3. Jesus is the only savior who can atone for our sins.
4. God can have no sin in Heaven, but through the crucifixion and resurrection of Jesus, our sins are forgiven.
5. We must choose to accept the gift or God's salvation.
6. While on the Earth, God has a worthy plan for each of us.
7. Ultimately, all Christians will be welcomed in Heaven.

God also gives all of us certain gifts, talents, and interests. We are expected to use these gifts, talents, and interests to serve others in support of the cause of Christ. (Romans 12:6–8) We must accept God's gifts and make the most of them while we are here. It is not always easy, but becomes easier when we who love God want to please Him. He encourages us with verses like Philippians 4:13 which says, *"I can do all things through Him who strengthens me."* And remember, Romans 8:28, where Paul reminds us, *"And we know that God causes all things to work together for good to those who love Him, to those who are called according to His purpose."* Another comforting verse for times when things don't seem to be going well is in Romans 8:31, *"If God is for us, who is against us?"*

Be of good cheer, and know that God is God, the Grand Architect and Creator of the universe, and He loves you.

#5
How Do I Find Truth to Guide My Life?

This is an essential question for those who wish to live meaningful and fulfilling lives on the Earth and beyond. Truth is essential for living a life of Godly works. Truthfulness is the foundation for relationships with God, Jesus, the Holy Spirit, and people. All Godly relationships involve trust, and trust requires truth. We cannot hope to live a righteous life without truth. God's Word is the only truth we can trust to guide us through the inevitable struggles and challenges of life in this fallen world. Sin entered when Adam and Eve yielded to Satan's temptation and sin has been part of the world since that time. If we depend upon ourselves to produce truth, we misguide ourselves. We live in fleshly bodies that are by nature self-centered and sinful, (Romans 6:19 and 7:25). But, praise God, we have hope to overcome our sins in God's eyes. The only good news about sin is that God gives us an avenue to have them forgiven.

As you know, In John 14:6 Jesus said, *"I am the way, and the truth, and the life; no one comes to the Father, but through me."* There are many man-made religions in the world, but salvation is only available through Jesus. In Acts 4:12 we learn, *"And there is salvation in no one else; for there is no other name under heaven that has been given among men; by which we must be saved."*

If we want to live a good life of abundance, God tells us to accept His Son, Jesus through baptism and we will have it abundantly, (John 10:10b). Of course, as followers of Jesus, we have an obligation to live by God's commandments, engage in His word so it becomes second nature to us, be obedient, and do good works. These works include serving the cause of Christ and following God's commandments and his great commission.

John, the disciple, tells us that we can know the truth and it comes from God. John 8:31–32 reads, *"Jesus therefore was saying to those Jews who had believed Him, 'If you abide in My word, then you are truly disciples of Mine; and you shall know the truth and the truth shall make you free.'"* This is God-given liberty which produces joy, praise, and gratefulness in us.

The Holy Spirit

It is a blessing that God provides Christians with His Holy Spirit to help us serve the cause of Christ. In John 16:13 Jesus said to His disciples, *"But when He, the spirit of truth comes, He will guide you in all the truth, for He will not speak on His own initiative, but whatever He hears, He will speak; and He will disclose to you what is to come."* That same spirit of God and truth takes up residence in Christians at their baptism. In Acts 2:38, Peter spoke to the repentant Jews in Jerusalem when they realized they had crucified the expected Messiah, Jesus, and asked *"What must we do?"* Peter replied, *"Repent and let each of you be baptized in the name of Jesus Christ for the forgiveness of your sins; and you shall receive the gift of the Holy Spirit."* Think about that. Baptized people have the Spirit of God dwelling in them to help them fulfill God's commandments and His great commission!

In his book, "The Spirit-filled Life," Charles Stanley spoke about how we can use the Holy Spirit's assistance. "The Holy Spirit is doing His work in your life every day. He doesn't need to change a thing. What needs to change is your awareness of His presence and activity." (24)

This is a Godly gift that only baptized Christians receive. I have often taught classes on this subject and inevitably someone asks, "How do we hear from the Holy Spirit?" My answer is simple, "Listen to Him." The Holy Spirit is a personality and He wants to do God's will in helping Christians. He wants us to be aware and receptive to His guidance.

Romans 8:1–2 provides assurance to all Christians stating, *"There is therefore now no condemnation to those who are in Christ Jesus. For the law of the spirit of the life in Christ Jesus has set you free from the law of sin and death."* The Holy Spirit is a great advocate, just as are God and our Savior Jesus.

Yes, Christians are sanctified (set apart) by God and His truth, but He invites everyone to be saved. As you know, God tells us that He has revealed Himself to all people since the creation. Consequently they are without excuse if they reject him and his eternal blessings. (Romans 1:19–20)

If you have read this far in this primer for making wise choices, you have really already learned how to find truth. Please treasure it and continue learning from scripture as fervently as a drowning person clings to a life preserver!

Chapter 3
Biblical Answers to Life's Questions I

#6

What Should I Do about Jesus?

This is the most important question each of us must ask. Each person on Earth who learns about Jesus must someday ask this question of himself or herself and come to an eternally important conclusion. The question must not be ignored or put off until later; it is the **ultimate choice**. Each of us should want to protect our soul, a precious gift of God. We can't depend on our relatives, friends, preachers, or teachers to be the experts on God's plan of salvation. We must eagerly work out our own future by learning what God says about it.

In the Gospel of Matthew 13:45–46 Jesus said, *"Again, the kingdom of heaven is like a merchant seeking fine pearls. And upon finding one pearl of great value, he went and sold all that he had, and bought it."* In this short parable, the pearl of great value represents the Kingdom of God. This Kingdom is the church established by Jesus and His apostles some two thousand years ago. The church is not a building, but the collective assembly of Christian converts throughout the world.

Each of us must decide whether to accept Jesus through baptism, as the Son of God and our Savior or reject Him and His saving grace. To ignore or delay the question is the same as rejecting Him.

Until now, we have mostly concentrated on God's gift of His Son and our salvation, the up side of this choice. At this point, however, we must see what the Bible says about those souls who reject the gift of Jesus and the Holy Spirit. Let's spend a few minutes looking at the down side of the choice.

Matthew 10:32–33 reads, *"Everyone therefore who shall confess me before men, I will also confess him before My Father who is in heaven. But whoever shall deny Me before men, I will also deny him before My Father who is in heaven."* It is clear that those who reject Jesus bring down God's justice upon them. Accept Jesus and heavenly blessings, including eternal life, are bestowed on you. Reject Jesus and you have chosen to have hellish things come to you. This is why I call accepting Christ as your Savior the **ultimate choice** for all of us.

In my experience, Satan has three big snares set for people who are trying to make the **ultimate choice**.

1. Satan's biggest snare is to appeal to people's pride to keep them from obeying God's will for them to accept his Son. Selfish pride keeps them from surrendering to His cause. This is one of the Devil's three big tricks, "the boastful pride of life," (1 John 3:16).

It is also important that we address two more big snares that the Devil, sometimes called the father of lies and the doubter, sets for people who are considering the **ultimate choice**, which is truly a life or death decision.

2. Satan's second snare is to convince us that we are too big a sinner to ever be accepted by Christ. I have had people tell me this very thing. What a tragedy. Satan tricks them into using their human guilt to convict themselves, instead of accepting God's mercy which was established completely when Jesus died on the cross for their sins. If God can love King David after his adulterous and murderous behavior, He can love and save you. If Jesus converted the murderous and persecuting Saul and turned him into Paul, the

most prolific evangelist in history, He can do the same for you, if you let him.

3. The third snare occurs after we have accepted Jesus and have been baptized. Over time, Satan continuously reminds us of our sordid past and sometimes we begin dwelling on those sins and become overwhelmed with past guilt. Remember, we tend to manifest those things we dwell on too much. The result is to doubt that we are fully saved and we begin to drift away from the only person/deity who can save us from our sins.

Don't make Jesus get back on the cross to absorb your sins a second time. He has already died for those sins and they are no longer in the memory of God, (Jeremiah 31:34b). Get them out of your memory, put forgiven sins behind you, and move forward in the cause of Christ.

In Philippians 3:13–14, the Apostle Paul says, *"Brethren, I do not regard myself as having laid hold of it yet, (the righteousness of faith and his resurrection from the dead); but one thing I do: forgetting what lies behind and reaching forward to what lies ahead. I press on toward the goal for the prize of the upward call of God in Christ Jesus."*

Here is a great quote with an unknown author that applies to Christians with this problem. "Never be a prisoner of your past. It was just a lesson, not a life sentence."

We can overcome the wiles of the Devil by looking at James 4:7 which reads, *"Submit therefore to God. Resist the Devil and he will flee from you!"* Essentially, we should avoid getting ourselves into sinful situations by recognizing who is behind the temptations and moving away from them. But the key to overcoming Satan is to surrender to God by accepting Jesus as our savior.

If you once knew and loved Jesus, but have fallen away, you can be restored by repenting and restoring a commitment to serve the cause of Christ. See 1 John 1:9 where John, a disciple of Jesus tells Christians that God will forgive their repented sins. The only truth that can be relied on to help you make your decision is in the Bible, and only you can make the choice to repent and reconcile with God.

As has been mentioned, when we can get over ourselves, surrender to Jesus, and ask for God's direction in our lives, we become truly free. We are Free from trying to please everyone, trying to be the best at everything, trying to discern truth from fiction, and presenting a false front of security and success to the world. When we drop the "world" as our measure of success, life gets more meaningful, liberating, exciting, and enjoyable!

When we commit ourselves totally to Jesus, we escape the bonds of the world and begin a pilgrimage of learning and supporting His cause more thoroughly so we can help lead wandering or wavering people to Him through the Word of God.

If you are still not sure of your **ultimate choice**, please remember that the best way to prepare yourself to answer this question is to pray to God for His guidance and hear and read scripture on the subject. When you pray, it must be with a sincere request for His help and guidance. You can begin to develop a relationship with our creator by praying with thanksgiving, belief, and expectation.

Attending a Bible-based church is a good first step if you do not already attend one. Reading the Bible for yourself is the best thing you can do. There are millions of good people who attend church, but have never read the word on their own. Seeking counsel from Godly people can be extremely useful, but only if they are well-versed on the subject and are living the loving life of a baptized Christian. Avoid seeking advice from non-believers, because they will consciously or unconsciously try to lead you away from Jesus since they have ignored Him or have rejected Him. Misery loves company.

In fact, the Bible addresses the company we should avoid. 1 Corinthians 5:11 reads, *"I wrote to you not to associate with any so-called brother if he is*

*an immoral person, or covetous, or an idolater, or a reviler, or a drunkard, or
a swindler-not even to eat with such a one."*

Author Allen Webster wrote a succinct tract titled "You Can't Get to
Heaven Alone" that counters the mistaken notion that we can get to
heaven without baptism. If you are thinking that being a good, faithful
person will get you into heaven without baptism, I recommend you read
this tract. It is listed in the References at the end of this publication.

John M. Hunt wrote a useful list of topical Bible verses titled *A Bookmark
of Basic Bible References*. This is a convenient tool for locating key
scriptures. There are also many other publications about choosing Jesus,
but there is no substitute for God's Word when trying to make the most
important decision in your life. No human author can present the whole
truth of God.

Most theologians and ministers recommend reading the four New
Testament Gospels that tell the good news that Jesus died for our sins.
These Gospel books are Matthew, Mark, Luke, and John. The Gospel
of John provides a clear understanding of who Jesus is, why He chose
to come to Earth in the form of man, what His purpose was, and what
He can do for you in this life and the next. I also recommend reading
the books of Romans and Colossians as you prepare to make a learned
decision. If you have already decided to accept Christ, I recommend you
also read or reread these six Bible books so you can be fully equipped to
lead others to Christ.

Please remember that man's interpretation of Biblical scripture is
sometimes wrong. As you read the Bible, be sure to interpret and
understand the text in the first century context in which it was written.
For example, the book of Revelation has often been equated to 20th and
21st century world politics and international prophesies when it was
clearly written to first century Christians about Roman oppression.

Biblical Evidence of Jesus

If you read the whole New Testament, under which we are living at this time, it is clear that every biblical conversion to Jesus, including the original 3,000 at Pentecost, were baptized. Even our Lord Jesus chose to be baptized by John the Baptist as an example to all mankind. It represents his death, burial, and resurrection.

Old Testament prophesies of the coming of Jesus as the Messiah, the Hebrew word for "the Chosen One," are abundant. The major prophet Isaiah described Jesus, His purpose, where He would be born, and how He would die, 700 years before it happened! (cf. Isaiah 53)

In Isaiah 7:14 we read: *"Therefore the Lord Himself will give you a sign: Behold, a virgin will be with child and bear a son, and she will call his name Immanuel* (God with us). In Zechariah 9:9 we are told, *"Rejoice greatly, O daughter of Zion! Shout in triumph, O daughter of Jerusalem! Behold, your king is coming to you. He is just and endowed with Salvation, humble and mounted on a donkey."*

More than 500 years later we are told in Luke 19:28–40, that Jesus rode a donkey into Jerusalem during the Passover the week before His crucifixion. There are many more specific prophesies about Jesus's coming and they were all fulfilled to the letter.

When we look at prophecies of the whole Bible, it is incredible how most have already been fulfilled and more are being fulfilled as the anticipation of Jesus's return gets closer. We previously referenced Hugh Ross's book, "Fulfilled Prophecy: Evidence for the Reliability of the Bible," where his research indicates that of the 2,500 Biblical prophecies, 2,000 have been fulfilled to the letter and the remaining 500 reach into the future. We have every reason to expect the last 500 prophecies will be fulfilled when Jesus returns to pronounce the judgment of people who have lived or are living on the Earth.

In addition to Biblical evidence, many ancient historians including the most prolific writer in Jesus's time, Josephus, wrote about Jesus. There are no denials that Jesus lived. But most Jewish people and Muslims believe he was just a significant Rabbi (teacher). They deny the deity of Jesus and the New Testament covenant in order to follow their traditional religious beliefs.

As you study the Bible and learn about Jesus and His saving grace, hopefully you will come to believe that Christ is your Savior. When this happens, the last question will become apparent. "What must I do to be saved?"

If you would like more researched evidence of Jesus, I encourage you to read the New Testament and consider reading the second edition of *Evidence That Demands a Verdict: Life-changing Truth for a Skeptical World* by Josh and Sean McDowell.

#7
What Must I Do to Be Saved?

Many good preachers have written about this question and one of them was my good Texan friend, Owen Cosgrove, a lifelong preacher and author. He wrote many books and tracts on Biblical topics and often quoted Matthew 28:18, where Jesus said, *"All authority has been given to me in heaven and on Earth."* Dr. Cosgrove would then state "Therefore, if we are to receive God's saving grace, we must do so on Christ's terms." He was an astute person, knowing that humans are often tempted to change God's prescription for salvation to more easily meet the convenience of the masses.

All humans are dead in sin unless there is a way to receive atonement for those sins. Solomon, the wisest human of his time, said in Ecclesiastes 12:14, *"For God will bring every deed into judgment, with every secret thing, whether good or evil."* Romans 6:23 states it clearly, *"For the wages of sin is death, but the free gift of God is eternal life in Christ Jesus our lord."* Praise be to God that He gave us Jesus, the perfect sacrificial lamb, as atonement for our sins. And God wants all of us to be baptized into Him for forgiveness, and we will receive the Holy Spirit to guide us through this life and into the next, Acts 2:38. But we have to make the **ultimate choice** of this life and the next to accept His invitation. How do we make this conversion of thought, action, and purpose?

Conversion happens when we choose to live for Jesus and be in the will of God rather than to be conformed to the world as explained in Romans 12:2, *"And do not be conformed to this world, but be transformed by the renewing of your mind, that you may prove what the will of God is, that which is good and acceptable and perfect."*

Once you are baptized by immersion, your name is listed in Jesus' Book of Life. In Revelation 21:27 we are told that only those written in the Lamb's Book of Life will enter the New Jerusalem (Heaven).

In John 3 we learn about Nicodemus, a ruler of the Jews, who came to Jesus by night and declared that he knew Jesus was from God for he could not be making miracles without God. Jesus replied in John 3:3 *"Truly, truly, I say to you that unless one is born again, he cannot see the Kingdom of God."* Nicodemus questioned how one could be born again and in v. 5 Jesus replied, *"Truly, truly I say to you, unless one is born of water and the spirit, he cannot enter into the kingdom of God."* Jesus was talking about immersion baptism and receiving the gift of the Holy Spirit that Peter declared in Acts 2:38.

In 1 Peter 3:21 we learn that we are saved by our commitment to Jesus Christ through baptism. *"And corresponding to that, baptism now saves you, not the removal of dirt from the flesh, but an appeal to God for a good conscience, through the resurrection of Jesus Christ."* We are all commanded to be baptized and to baptize believers ourselves in the great commission of Jesus in Matthew 29:19, 20.

The Holy Bible tells us that we should believe in Jesus, as did the Philippian jailer and his family, in Acts 16:31–33. Those new converts first heard the word, were converted to Christ, and were baptized.

The Greek word *baptizo* means immersion as do the Hebrew words *tevilah* and *mikveh*. Most of the Bible was originally written in these two languages.

There are many unwise religious denominations that originally baptized converts by immersion, but later, their leaders decided to change their original practice and adopted sprinkling or pouring water on the heads of people as baptism. Some even sprinkle the heads of babies. There are no verses or examples of these practices in the Bible.

Lately many churches have eliminated baptism altogether and preach that "faith only" can save mortals. This human idea that we don't need to be baptized and "faith only" is all that is needed for salvation is also not substantiated in the Bible.

Today we often see television promotions by well-meaning church leaders who encourage people to simply say the "sinner's prayer" and they will be saved. They explain that the "sinner's prayer" is a repentant prayer with a request to be saved and a pledge to serve the cause of Christ. This ill-advised practice, which began by a few evangelists in the late 1800s, has become so popular, even some Bible-based research books subscribe to this unbiblical suggestion. It may be more convenient, but this life or death spiritual decision is far too important to trust men rather than God, (Psalm 118:8).

For example, many of these "faith only" advocates point to Revelation 3:20 as Biblical support, *"Behold, I stand at the door and knock; if anyone hears My voice and opens the door, I will come into him, and dine with him, and he with Me."* These advocates lift this verse out of context. Jesus is not talking to unbaptized people, He is talking to Christians from the church of Laodicea. Author and Minister Michael Shank says in his book, *Muscle and a Shovel*, "The sinner's prayer is the greatest hoax on mankind." (367)

Jesus Himself chose to be baptized by immersion as an example for us to surrender ourselves and symbolically experience His death, burial, and resurrection. Jesus did not have to be baptized, but He chose to do it as an example for how lost people can be saved.

Don't misunderstand this critical part of your salvation. It is clearly expressed in Romans 6:3–5, *"Or do you not know that all of us who have been baptized into Christ Jesus have been baptized into His death? Therefore, we have been buried with Him through baptism into death, in order that as Christ was raised from the dead through the glory of the Father, so we too might walk in newness of life. For if we have become united with Him in the likeness of His death, certainly we shall be also in the likeness of His resurrection."*

Many scriptures in the New Testament clearly give us the pattern for accepting Jesus's salvation through immersion baptism and each of us should review the Bible ourselves regarding this **ultimate choice** for eternity. In Philippians 2:12–13, the apostle Paul told the Philippian Christians to *"work out your salvation with fear and trembling for it is God who is at work in you, both to will and to work for His good pleasure."*

When Philip was led by the Holy Spirit to teach the Ethiopian eunuch about Jesus, the eunuch saw much water and asked if he could be baptized. As recorded in Acts 8:37–39, *"And Philip said, "If you believe with all your heart, you may." And he answered and said, "I believe that Jesus Christ is the Son of God." And he (Philip) ordered the chariot to stop; and they both went down into the water. Philip as well as the eunuch, and he baptized him."*

People have often asked me what happens to people who have no access to baptism. They produce hypothetical examples, such as a man is dying from a car accident and repentantly reaches out to God for salvation before he dies. We are not given Biblical examples for all hypothetical situations, but I know our God is fair and just. He will handle those things according to His grace and truth. But the real question to be asked in these discussions, is why do you delay? When you decide to be baptized, you can be assured that God has led you to that conclusion, because He alone adds to His number of saved people, (Acts 2:47).

Indeed, Jesus sacrificed His life for us, even though He was without sin. It is important to understand from Him what we must do to be saved. Mark 16:16 records what Jesus said to His disciples just before he ascended to Heaven, *"He who has believed and has been baptized shall be saved, but he who has disbelieved shall be condemned."* This is a very clear message.

We must:

1. Hear (learn) about Jesus, our Savior, Romans 10:14.
2. Believe Jesus is our savior, there are no others, John 14:6.
3. Repent of our sins knowing that *"all have sinned and fall short of the Lord,"* Romans 3:23 and *"For the wages of sin is death, but the free gift of God is eternal life in Christ Jesus our Lord,"* Romans 6:23.
4. Confess our belief that Jesus is the Son of God and our Savior, Romans 10:10.
5. Be baptized by immersion as Jesus demonstrated, John 3:1–5, Acts 2:38; 8:34–39.
6. Stay faithful to our God for the rest of our lives, 2 Timothy 3:14.

Once you surrender yourself to the Lord's service and are baptized, your sins will no longer be remembered, Hebrews 8:12, and you will receive the gift of the Holy Spirit. You have then been converted. Conversion means to change, especially in the self-centered way we naturally think, which leads to a servant-oriented change of heart and attitude. You are then a member of God's kingdom on Earth and later, in heaven. And you are no longer alone. His spirit enters in you the moment you are baptized. Incredible!

Any committed Christian who was baptized may baptize you. Also, any Christian preacher who believes in the necessity of immersion baptism, will be happy to learn about your commitment to serve Jesus. They should be pleased to baptize you as well. In the Gospel of Luke 15:10 we are told that angels rejoice over the repentance of sinners! It is comforting that angelic beings in heaven rejoice over our conversions.

After Baptism

As you read and learn more from the Bible, you will discover that as a new or renewed Christian, your life on this Earth will improve in immeasurable ways. You will have life and have it more abundantly. (John 10:10b) You will have faith in God, Jesus, and the Holy Spirit, creators of the universe. You will receive joy by helping others and doing things that support the cause of Christ. Angels will minister to you as we are told in Hebrews 1:14. It is an amazingly meaningful and fulfilling experience. And the more you learn His word and do His will, the more you will be blessed. Here is a list of some of the new characteristics you will receive after baptism:

1. You are now a member of the assembly of Christ, often described as the Kingdom of God on Earth.
2. You no longer seek to serve yourself, rather you seek to serve Christ by sharing the Gospel with others and serving their needs.
3. You will hopefully stay in His word and remain faithful by joining a Godly assembly and studying His word.
4. If you hear false teaching, you will be quick to respectfully defend your faith in God's word.
5. You are now listed in the Lamb's Book of Life.
6. The Holy Spirit now dwells in you and guides you toward righteousness.

It is advisable to read your Creator's word every day to increase your relationship with Him, Jesus, and the Holy Spirit. This will become one of the most beneficial gifts you'll ever give to yourself and your family! In Colossians 3:16 we are told, *"Let the word of Christ richly dwell within you. With all wisdom teaching and admonishing one another with psalms and hymns and spiritual songs, singing with thankfulness in your hearts to God."* I highly recommend reading and rereading the book of Colossians, especially chapter three, to remind you to whom you belong and how to emerge as a new person in Christ.

Life will get far more exciting. As you know from Proverbs 16:9, we can make plans, but Jesus will choose our steps and we never know what He will want us to do next! And you will lose all fear of death, because those in Christ will live eternally with him. We sleep one moment and wake up in Paradise until we are taken to heaven after Christ's final judgment.

Upon baptism, you will realize that the Holy Spirit now dwells in you. As already mentioned, you are no longer alone in the world. He is your divine spiritual guide through this earthly journey. You will get to know and appreciate Him well as you learn to listen to Him. You will also be prepared to testify to your faith in Jesus.

The disciple, Peter, told Christians in 1 Peter 3:15 that they should be prepared to make a defense for their faith in Jesus and explain the hope that is in them. The best way to do that is to learn Biblical scriptures because they will sustain themselves and the Bible's truth. As we defend our faith to others, we must do it gently and patiently.

Faith, Hope, and Love

You will find that Christians have reason to receive and treasure **Faith**, **Hope**, and **Love**. These virtues are Godly and His word and the Holy Spirit help us grow strong in all three of these blessings. We read in 1 Corinthians 13:13, *"But now abide in faith, hope, love, these three, but the greatest of these s love."*

The virtue of **faith** represents trust in God, Jesus, the Word, and the Holy Spirit. It is an essential characteristic of people who choose to follow Jesus. True faith cannot be shaken, even when times are bad. In fact, we all experience bad times and that is especially true when we need to hold onto our faith to get us through our problems. People without faith are also without real hope.

The Open Bible (NASB) by Thomas Nelson Publishers, provides what I think is an excellent list of why faith is so important in Christians' lives:

1. Faith is our shield of protection because we know to whom we belong, Ephesians, 6:16.
2. We cannot be saved without faith, John 3:36.
3. We cannot be victorious in the world without faith, 1 John 4:4–6.
4. We cannot please God without faith, Hebrews 11:6.
5. We cannot have joy without faith, 1 Peter 1:8.
6. We are justified by faith, Galatians 2:16.

The virtue of **hope** represents those things you expect to occur. As a child, you expected your mother to feed you because she did it consistently. You looked forward to her meals and hoped she would keep delivering them. Hope provides a positive and optimistic outlook on life. Other people are attracted to this characteristic in you and will ask about it. That's your opportunity to witness to them about the source of your hope and faith.

The virtue of **love** represents the most prominent characteristic of God. In 1 John 4:16, we read, *"And we have come to know and have believed the love which God has for us. God is love, and the one who abides in love abides in God, and God abides in him."* People recognize Godly people for their compassion and ability to forgive trespasses by others. Godly people strive to become love, personified.

In summary all three of these wonderful virtues are eternally beneficial for spreading the Gospel of Christ and they are immediately beneficial for those who live by them, because we reap what we sow as described in Galatians 6:7. We will examine this critical concept in Chapter Three.

#8
What Kind of Spouse and Career Should I Seek?

There are two earthly questions that all of us must consider, especially young people. These are practical questions because we must live in this World. All of us want to be successful in our marriage and our careers. Let's see what the Bible says about choosing a spouse.

Proverbs 18:22 states that Christians should not be unequally yoked together and there is no communion between light and darkness. God clearly favors marriage and says it is a blessing. He created the union between men and women from the very beginning with Adam and Eve. In Genesis 2:24 we are told, *"For this cause a man shall leave his father and his mother, and shall cleave to his wife; and they shall become one flesh."* God also values the family unit as is evident in many places in the Bible, especially in Psalm 128. Indeed, God planted families as the foundation unit of civilization on the Earth. Churches and families are the well springs of moral teaching in the lives of succeeding generations.

We also have an obligation to support ourselves and our families and communities and we need good careers to produce the funding so we can provide that support. We also hope to work, enjoy, and excel in our chosen career field. A rewarding career is one of the blessings of life on Earth, if we choose well, work hard, and see it as a way to serve God.

The Bible informs us that work is part of God's plan for us. In Genesis 2:15, we are told that God put Adam in the garden to cultivate it. In Proverbs 10:4 we learn that a slack hand causes poverty, but a diligent hand produces wealth. In most Biblical stories and parables, the characters are described by their work. Lydia, the first Christian convert in Europe, was a seller of purple cloth which was very costly and was the preferred color of royalty. Consider references to the rich young ruler, the Shepherd, the tax collector, and most disciples were fisherman.

In Genesis 1:28, God blessed Adam and Eve and told them, *"Be fruitful and multiply, and fill the earth, and subdue it; and rule over the fish of the sea and over the birds of the sky, and over every living thing that moves on the earth."* We also realize that in this world, there are no perfect jobs, but our attitudes are entirely controlled by us. Colossians 3:3 says, *"Whatever you do, do your work heartily as for the Lord rather than men."* This verse has aided me more than any other as I learned to work heartily, oftentimes with ungodly people. Finding a career in your field of talent and interest will be a blessing. If you love your work, it is a great way to do meaningful things and get paid for it. Proverbs 16:3 advises that we should commit to the Lord whatever we do and he will establish our plans.

As a lifelong educator, I encourage you to consider taking a career aptitude test to get an idea of what you are naturally inclined to like. But in the end, make the decision about your career field with both your mind and your heart. If you decide later that you are unsatisfied with your career choice, change it and get the credentials you will need for the next one. Remember Philippians 4:13, *"I can do all things through Christ who strengthens me."* The more your thoughts become intertwined with scripture, your career success, abundance, happiness, and fulfillment are now dependent on your thoughts, attitude, and skills.

We Christians should be happy and confident, not arrogant, in our work as we keep our thoughts, emotions, and intentions in concert with God's Word. Biblical scripture is truth and during Jesus's Sermon on the Mount above the Sea of Galilee, He said in Matthew 7:7, *"Ask, and it shall be given unto you; seek, and you shall find; knock, and it shall be opened to you."* We Christians are destined to succeed, here and in the hereafter, if we are in God's will. Be bold in your service to Jesus by asking in prayer, seeking with thoughts, and knocking on new doors of opportunity!

And whatever type of work you choose to do, please do it with enthusiasm! Most people gravitate toward and appreciate enthusiastic people. We are advised in Matthew 5:16 to, *"Let your light shine before men in such a way that they may see your good works and glorify your Father who is in heaven."*

The Greek word for enthusiasm is *entheos* which means being "in or with God." This is sound, Godly advice for career success in my experience. If we are "in or with God," how could we not be enthusiastic?

In our next chapter, we will examine one of God's most important and immutable laws that pertains to every human, saved or unsaved. This law can be classified as good, bad, or ugly depending upon whether we ignore it or work with it for good or bad outcomes. But, once you understand this most fundamental and universal law, life in this world gets much easier and more fun to navigate. Turn up the lights and clear your head. This next chapter is a revealing treasure hunt!

Chapter 4
God's Universal Law

A fter accepting Christ and being baptized, we are still living on this Earth which is filled with good and evil. The spiritual battle between these two contrasting principles continues from antiquity. Gaining an understanding of the most essential law of the universe is critical for making good decisions and living in contentment.

Jesus often told parables during His ministry on Earth. Parables have been described as earthly stories with heavenly meanings. One of my favorites is about the wheat and the tares. It is told in Matthew 13:24–30. Jesus opened that parable by saying the Kingdom of heaven may be compared to a man who sowed wheat in his field, but in the night, his enemy sowed tare seeds (weeds) in among the wheat seeds. When the wheat sprung up so did the tares, and the field hands discovered this evil deed. They asked the owner if he wanted them to pull out the tares, but the owner said no because in the formative period, both plants looked alike and they would be unknowingly pulling up wheat also. The owner told them to let both grow together until the harvest. At harvest time, the field hands first gathered the tares because they bore no grain, bundled them, and threw them into the fire. Afterwards, they reaped the wheat and put it into the barn.

This parable demonstrates that evil is in this world. It means that we Christians and non-Christians are living among each other. In 1 John 5:19 we confirm this truth, *"We know that we are of God, and the whole world lies in the power of the evil one."* The harvest, or final judgment by Jesus, will determine where people end up. He will separate not only the wheat from the tares, but the saved from the unsaved by the laws of

God. In the meantime, be aware that evil and uninformed people are all around us. It is up to us to help spread the light of Christ to help Him save those who are lost.

Justice, often called judgment, is a fixed law of the universe that ultimately separates righteous people from wicked people. Unlike the world that harbors both saved and unsaved people, heaven can only accept saved people to share a home with God. As has already been mentioned, Jesus himself will someday return to the Earth and separate saved souls from unsaved souls, (John 5:22–24; Romans 14:10).

On several occasions I have had non-believers ask how our loving and merciful God could condemn people to hell. They don't understand that God doesn't condemn them to hell, they condemn themselves by making bad choices such as rejecting God, Jesus, and the Holy Spirit.

Cause and Effect

In this worldly life, we humans are unaware of many things in the universe and our planet. Scientists are still trying to identify and explain the laws of physics. The one great Godly universal law that affects our current physical existence and spiritual existence is the rule of **"Cause and Effect."** This ubiquitous and immutable truth is applicable in every dimension of our universe and our lives. This rule also affects all living things including celestial planets, stars, moons, and suns in the universe that we know about and those unknown bodies yet to be discovered. Nothing we think, hope, or believe will change this law. It is impartial and there are no exceptions. God confirmed this law in the frequent occasions that He told us about it in his word or illustrated it in Biblical examples and parables.

In Paul's letter to the Galatians in Chapter 6:7, 9 we are told, *"Do not be deceived, God is not mocked, for whatever a man sows, this he will also reap."* What we sow in this life is the *cause* of what we reap, which is the *effect*. Our God created us as free-willed souls equipped to think and reason for ourselves. He gave us the intelligence to think and reason within ourselves to make good choices. But He also gave us His word as a full measure of truth to help us draw the right conclusions in every decision we make.

In Jesus' parable of the sower of seed, we can more fully understand God's support as we make difficult decisions. In Matthew chapter 13 Jesus tells a multitude of people that a sower cast his seeds on the ground and some fell beside the road and birds ate them. Others fell on rocky places and could not grow to harvest. Other seeds fell among thorns and were strangled by the vines. Yet some fell on good soil and produced a great crop of grain. Jesus later explained to his disciples that the seed is God's word and some people don't receive it, others receive it, but can't understand it, and others receive it, understand it and live by it to produce much fruit.

God's word is a seed. It can only replicate or produce itself. As we struggle to make decisions, we should use the seeds of scripture which represent truth in making our decisions. This is how we can be assured that we are bearing fruit with our lives. We should also pray to our God with supplications for guidance. With difficult decisions, it is advisable to read relevant scripture, do your best, pray about it, (*cause*) and let God do the rest (*effect*). His word bears goodness.

God's law of cause and effect is fair and measurable in all that we think and do. We are expected to be responsible for our choices and actions. We are captains of our own ship, and we have the spiritual blessings of God and the Holy Spirit to call upon to help us make good choices. However, we must first learn how to control and guide our ship through prayer, meditation, and clear-minded thoughts. Then we can take the tiller and steer a steady course through the rough and calm seas of our lives.

With practice, we can learn to pursue righteousness and steer ourselves through life with the right thoughts and choices. These thoughts and choices gain focus through prayer, by following scripture, loving God and others, and accepting and loving Christ.

But what happens when someone never learns to steer the ship in the first place, or they don't have the Godly resources of Christians? He or she can take the tiller of their lives, but if they are not prepared to guide it properly, shipwrecks are inevitable.

And what do you suppose happens if a Christian is trained to guide the ship, but is distracted or tempted and removes his or her hand from the ship's tiller?

You might have noticed that I said we can learn to *pursue* righteousness. Only Jesus had full righteousness on Earth. The difficulty is that our bodies are made of flesh which is corruptible and susceptible to sinful behaviors. Even the apostle Paul in his letter to the Philippians 3:12–14 said that he had not yet attained resurrection from death and was not already perfected: but he pressed on toward the call of Jesus. This is Godly wisdom at work, when He keeps us humble and thankful for His blessings. Free will requires that we stay focused and faithful to whom we belong, Jesus, and our ship will stay on course.

Unfortunately, Satan is always roaring about seeking whom he might devour. (1 Peter 5:8) But, as my church Elder friend William Ireland often says, Satan only has three main tricks in his bag to distract us. These are revealed in 1 John 3:17, *"For all that is in the world, the love of the flesh and the lust of the eyes and the boastful pride of life, is not from the Father, but is from the world."* We are all faced with choices for good or evil. Of course, the evil is always camouflaged so we can more easily justify our conscience when choosing it to satisfy some temptation. Fortunately, the more we know God's Word and understand His law of cause and effect, the easier it becomes to recognize satanic temptations and make good choices.

This universal law of **cause and effect** is fast in place on the earth and in heavenly places. When Lucifer, once described as the bright morning star, yielded to temptation to overthrow God (cause), he and his demons were thrown from heaven to the Earth (effect).

We are all tempted almost continuously, but we Christians have it in our power to see temptations for what they are, consider the consequences, and, as you have heard in James 4:7, be in God and resist the Devil. Please note that we must first be submissive and have a relationship with God before our resistance to Satan and his temptations will be effective. In this example, Satan's temptations are the *cause* and our resistance with the help of God, is the *effect*, including a fleeing Devil!

Of course we all sin. Even Christians stumble and yield to the wiles of the Devil. As long as we live in fleshly bodies, we will be struggling with the challenge between our flesh and our soul or spirit. (Galatians 5:15) But we Christians know we can honestly repent of our transgressions, and when we ask for forgiveness, it is granted because He listens to our prayers. Proverbs 15:29 reads, *"The Lord is far from the wicked. But He hears the prayer of the righteous."*

Our Thoughts Determine Our Destiny

Now, let's look at this universal law a little deeper. All choices have consequences, and being in harmony with Jesus is the best predictor for making good decisions. One great way to keep yourself in harmony with our Savior, is to consider the law of cause and effect with each decision, especially impactful decisions. Basically, ask yourself what is the up side and down side of the decision you are considering. Ask yourself if the decision you are favoring is in agreement with God's Word which is Jesus. God's word is described as Jesus Himself in John 1:14a which says, *"And the word became flesh and dwelt among us…"* Our thoughts, which drive our choices, are the *cause* and what we ultimately decide produces the *effect* of that decision.

Our choices cause good or bad consequences. Therefore, it is important to first identify the source of unimpeachable truth to insure that our choices about living are based on truth, not lies. In this case, we have it easier than hundreds of generations before us. The Christian Bible, is the only source of divine and eternal truth. The fearsome beauty of our free will, which produces His great law of cause and effect, is that we are held responsible for ourselves. Fortunately, we Christians have the ability to filter our choices through the help of almighty God, His word (Jesus), and the Holy Spirit.

As I have mentioned, thoughts are things, the essence of consciousness which we call life. Like everything else, thoughts emit energy as frequencies oscillating in the universe that cause our thoughts to manifest themselves, whether good or bad. We can learn to use our thoughts for positive or negative growth. God said he spoke the universe into existence. Genesis Chapter 1 tells how God "spoke" the universe into being which came from His thoughts. Psalm 33:6 says, *"By the word of the Lord, the heavens were made."* And Psalm 33:9 says, *"For He spoke, and it was done; He commanded and it stood fast."*

Wise people are discerning with what they choose to think about, because that is what begins to drive them into action. Our thoughts soon come out of our mouths and are put into action. In effect, we cause our own destiny through our minds and what we choose to think about and speak about.

To have a life of joy, purpose, and meaning, think joyful, purposeful, and meaningful thoughts. Be conscious of and reflect on the positive words and lessons that come from God, rather than the temptations of this world, and you will grow into a contented and happy child of God.

We have been blessed by our creator with the opportunity to develop our own attitude about life and other people. We alone choose the attitude we project. Many books have been written on this subject and almost all agree that each person is responsible for his or her attitude. Millions of people resist this idea and blame their negative attitudes on "the way life has treated them so unfairly." I was honored to serve on Zig Ziglar's corporate board for eight years. In the last half of the 20th century he was the most popular American author and platform speaker on the value of positive thinking. He was fond of saying, "It's not what happens to us, but how we choose to respond to it that is important." Don't be fooled, each of us chooses our own attitude each day.

The late Henry Ford's familiar quote can summarize this topic. He was fond of saying, "If you think you can or think you can't, you're right!" We do ourselves a favor by consciously and intentionally adopting positive and cheerful attitudes. We Christians in particular should have positive attitudes because we have God's promises, the Holy Spirit's guidance, and the eternal salvation of Jesus. In Hebrews 1:14, we learn that even angels minister to us!

Interacting with Others

God wants no one to perish, (2 Peter 3:9). We will do well to remember that God loves all the people He creates and we should do our best to recognize that all people are His creations. This is easier said than done in some cases, but getting along with people is a very righteous and beneficial skill.

You have probably heard about the "Golden Rule." Parents use it as an admonition to their children to treat everyone the way they wish to be treated. It is found in Matthew 7:12, *"Therefore, however you want people to treat you, so treat them, for this is the Law and the Prophets."* This fundamental moral and ethical admonition emanated from the Bible. God provides an instruction manual for getting along with others in beneficial ways. We reap what we sow, for example, is a profound piece of Biblical advice that demonstrates the law of cause and effect.

As we progress through life, we should recognize that each person is influenced by a unique set of circumstances that influenced his or her concept of themselves. We are all products of our environment which includes family, community, culture, exposure to religion, education, and a broad host of direct experiences as we grow into adults. We are also affected by the financial, health, and moral conditions of the family. We are also influenced by suggestions from others whom we admire, and our perceptions of ourselves evolve as we move toward adulthood. Schools and churches, mosques, or synagogues also deeply influence who we have become and how we think. Fortunately, as we have discussed, God has wired us to seek Him.

The Bible also encourages us to associate with good people, especially other Christians, and warns us not to socialize with evil people except for sharing our walk with Christ or providing them with kindness. In 1 Corinthians 15:33 we are warned: *"Do not be deceived, bad company corrupts good morals."*

One of the most moving parables in the Bible, the Prodigal Son, illustrates this truth in human nature, (Luke 15:11–32). In this famous parable, the youngest son of a good Jewish farmer seeks and receives an early inheritance from his father. He journeys to a foreign land where he relishes in the evilness of the world. His money soon runs out, his pseudo friends abandon him, and he has to take a job tending swine, which to Jewish people is sinful. He is literally starving and decides to return home, hoping to serve his father as a laborer. The father sees him from afar and runs to accept his son back into the household. This story reveals the mercy of God. When straying people repent and return to Him, there is joy in Heaven, (Luke 15:7).

It is perfectly human to be egocentric. Just look at any two-year-old child and you will confirm this truth about human nature. However, as we mature, God, through His word, gives us a chance to grow beyond ourselves and serve a much greater cause. As we age, even in this fallen world, we learn that the righteous traits of love, faith, hope, humility, kindness, forgiveness, and compassion become the characteristics that are most preferred by others and ordained by God. These virtues are spiritual in nature which help us overcome Satan's temptations of the flesh and the pride of life.

There is a humorous homily about human imperfections that says, "Jesus accepts us just the way we are, but He loves us too much to keep us that way." As we grow in Christ and the word, we are helping our spirits and minds to overcome egotism, fleshly desires, and unruly emotions. In this way we mature in Christ and become more Godly in our nature by learning to love others like we love ourselves.

Emotional Selves

Our emotional selves play a key role in our development. People desire and reward others who have learned to govern themselves. These wise people learn to think about their emotional reactions before they are expressed. They also learn to make reasoned responses by first carefully considering the *cause* and *effect* of every circumstance.

In the 1990s young American Christians wisely wore their "What Would Jesus Do" bracelets to remind themselves to consult Jesus with difficult decisions or temptations. People who think about Biblical scripture and righteous things can more easily control their negative or unflattering emotions. Don't always trust your emotions, especially if they are ungodly.

Of course, our emotions can be very useful. We praise a baby's first smile or first steps to reinforce their self-esteem and to encourage continued growth. Fortunately there is at least one great equalizer among all people and that is the free will to be kind, compassionate, and loving to others. In these and similar circumstances, it is virtuous to release your emotions generously.

Yes, thoughts are things, but they also are affected by and often originated from the law of cause and effect. As mentioned before, wise people challenge themselves to think in righteous, and not evil ways.

Spiritual Selves

Our spiritual selves play a bigger role as we learn more about how to release ourselves from the confines of a self-centered, worldly existence. When we learn to consistently think about others and their well-being before ourselves, our spirit is practicing God's wisdom and righteousness. When we consciously choose to do good works in the cause of Christ, we are maturing spiritually. Whenever we are tempted to criticize someone, but we choose to see things from their point of view, we are growing spiritually. One of my favorite preachers learned to avoid judging anyone, but he would occasionally observe that a self-centered person "appeared not to be fully developed yet." I think he was pretty well developed spiritually for living in this world.

A wise nineteenth century Frenchman, Pierre Teilhard de Chardin summed it up with his quote, "We are not humans having a spiritual experience, we are spirits having a human experience." The more you think of yourself as a spiritual being, the easier it becomes to govern your physical being. Our spiritual and thinking selves should dominate our physical and emotional selves.

As we absorb and practice His word, we begin to realize that the power to make us what we wish to become is within each of us. By possessing free will, we have the power to think our way into success as God defines it, from a world view to a spiritual view. This is especially true after we are baptized into Christ and receive the gift of the Holy Spirit who helps us grow in Christ.

Whether we recognize it or not, we are dealing with God's physical laws and His spiritual laws. His physical laws come from His physical creation of the universe and we can learn the basics about this vast subject through experience, others, science, and from the Bible. But His spiritual laws come directly through His word. If your desire is to grow spiritually, choose to study and follow His word.

Thinking is the primary activity of our spirit. Honesty or dishonesty are spiritual choices, as are morality or immorality, truth or lies, optimism or pessimism, and love or hate. Each of these contrasting couplets have the same *cause* and *effect* that is sometimes called the Principal of Reciprocity. Honesty yields honesty, dishonesty yields dishonesty, truth yields truth, lies beget lies, and love yields love. Many scriptures reveal that sin always produces punishment and goodness always produces reward. The universal law of *cause* and *effect* is everywhere and always at work.

We really do reap what we sow. We cannot honestly blame anyone but ourselves for our condition or our attitude. If we wish for a better condition in life, we must learn to make honest, truthful, and love-centered thoughts and choices. We can't hide our thoughts or choices from God, His law, or ourselves.

In the next chapter, we will explore our physical universe and learn some of what God says about it. Having a basic understanding of the universe is necessary if we hope to navigate in it well. It is interesting that God revealed many of His creation secrets in the Bible, sometimes thousands of years before human science discovered them!

Chapter 5

A Quick Look at His Universe

A s with all things, we should first see what God has said about the universe. Genesis 1:1 says, *"In the beginning God created the heavens and the earth."* This statement establishes that He is God, the creator of Heaven and Earth. Throughout the first chapter of Genesis, He demonstrates how He created day and night, and the seas and land. In the second chapter He made the universe for humans. In addition to Genesis, there are many other verses that describe His universe. You might consider looking at Psalm 33:6, Psalm chapter 19, Hebrews 11:3, Isaiah chapter 40, and Romans 4:17.

God called the universe and all its living creatures and plants into being through His thoughts and voice. God was the *cause* and the universe was the *effect* of His will.

There are physical laws that affect the universe among which are gravity, electromagnetism, nuclear force, relativity, and light. As I have briefly mentioned, there are also spiritual laws of contrasts like love and hate, good and evil. God has established a clear set of behavioral laws based on His morals and ethics. We are also affected by these laws and others that interconnect everything in the universe, sometimes referred to as the Law of Oneness. Few people think about this, but our free will with thoughts, words, and actions affect ourselves, the world, and the people in it.

The Bible also describes parts of the universe in language that first century humans could easily understand. For example, in Isaiah 40:22, God says, *"It is He that sitteth on the circle of the earth."* The Earth is round, but most humans thought it was flat until Aristotle pronounced, around 330 BC, that the Earth was round and the Greek mathematician, Eratosthenes, proved it in 240 BC.

Scientific Progress

We humans are continuing to make scientific progress in understanding the universe. For example, we were unaware of germs until the 19th century. Sub-atomic matter, the electromagnetic spectrum, quantum physics, the transistor, automobiles, airplanes and radio and television did not arrive until the 20th century. Computers, the Internet, space exploration, and artificial intelligence are booming in the 21st century and the human race is making unforeseen progress in understanding our physical environment. Yet, we still cannot scientifically explain how gravity, a critical element for life, works. We can explain the effects of it, but not the cause.

Several years ago I read a fascinating book on Quantum Physics research that observed on the microscopic level, that order naturally comes from chaos. I was not surprised. God's universe must follow His laws of mass, space, gravity, and time. Jesus knows what all it takes to hold everything together in an orderly fashion because Colossians 1:17 confirms this. The universe must be an orderly system both physically and spiritually.

Some 20th-century scientists suggested a cataclysmic celestial explosion must have created the universe, but they have failed to explain how a random "Big Bang" could create the universe and all the life that is in it. These evolutionists continue to ignore our true Creator, but have not discovered any reliable evidence of evolution from one species to another.

Scientists use their scientific method of analyzing how the universe works, but often fail to understand how, why, or who created it. Medical researchers have learned a plethora of important information about how to treat diseases, but many illnesses are still incurable. Dr. Francis Collins led a team of scientists in the genome project who made many discoveries in their breakthrough microbiology research. They also found more things they did not know existed that need to be studied. They discovered and mapped the microscopic essence of human life, DNA, but their research doesn't explain where that life came from or how it was created.

I have heard two presentations by Dr. Collins and both times he concluded that the complex nature of our chromosomes had to be thoughtfully created. At a large gathering of Christians in Charlotte, North Carolina, on December 10, 2024, Dr. Collins, a scientist and physician, also said that he did not receive any religious training as a child and he decided to be an atheist. But at age 27 he accepted Christ. He was stimulated to face the **ultimate choice** by an elderly patient who asked him what he believed. He said he could not answer the question. The more he sought all the answers from science, the more he realized that, "Science provided the evidence of God which I needed to understand before I could contemplate religion."

As observed before, the Holy Scriptures revealed many of the unknown questions about the universe thousands of years before people finally verified them through science. There are cosmic laws that hold celestial bodies in specific orbital pathways. Our Earth hangs in space spinning at a constant speed and tilted at a perfect angle necessary to support life. Job 26:7 states, *"He (God) stretches out the north over empty space. And hangs the earth on nothing."*

The Earth revolves around the sun every 365 days at the same speed. At the molecular level, the atoms within a molecule have a specific vibration rate and almost everything in the universe has similar oscillations. If any of these laws of physics were to slip out of rhythm with the rest of the universe, it is speculated that the whole universe would be adversely affected. Do you think our universe was an accident or was it intentionally created? Dr. Collins says God is the supreme mathematician and physicist.

In today's world there is much concern about the Earth remaining habitable by humans. In the 1970s many people feared a new ice age was imminent. In the 1990s many people reversed their fears from freezing to global warming. There are also science fiction movies about cataclysmic celestial disasters like when the Earth slips from its orbit or some other scary circumstance. Rest assured that the Earth and the universe will be fine until God has no more need of them. How do I know? Here is comforting assurance in Colossians 1:17, *"And He (Jesus) is before all things, and in Him all things hold together."* This doesn't mean we should abuse our environment, because we are obligated to take care of His creation. For example, the Earth was created with an automatic oxygen restoration system, but we realized that a limit on deforestation needed to be a global priority to provide adequate oxygen through photosynthesis. Eight major countries have agreed to address this important environmental issue.

It is interesting that God's creation and man's scientific research complement each other. As scientists discover new properties in microbiology and new cosmic laws about mass, space, gravity, and time, they are confirming some of the amazing things that Biblical scripture said He created thousands of years ago.

Yes, we are making scientific progress in understanding the universe and its laws, and this is good, especially since the gap between creation and science is narrowing. But it begs the question: What progress are we making toward helping the human race accept the atonement of Christ and commit to God's purposes?

Spiritual Progress

Archaeological and historical research have provided evidence that from the time humans existed, they worshiped beings higher than they perceived themselves to be. They worshiped stones, the sun, the moon, mythical beings, and unknown gods because they had a yearning to revere the Creator and they did not have God's Divine Scripture to guide them.

Several Biblical verses point out that all humans have a need to worship God. Psalm 42:1 reads, *"Just like a deer that craves streams of water, my whole being craves you (God)."* This is reminiscent of Romans 1:19–20 that says God has shown people Himself and they are without excuse if they don't pursue Him, (Romans 1:20).

Fortunately, the universal and only God, the Designer and Creator of the universe, reveals Himself to all of us through His Prophets, His Word, (His Son), the Holy Spirit, and through faithful Christians.

John, the youngest original disciple of Jesus, was inspired by the Holy Spirit to write in John 1:1, *"In the beginning was the word and the word was with God, and the word was God."* In John 1:14 the mystery of that verse is explained, *"The word became flesh and dwelt among us."* This Jesus, Son of God, was the co-creator of the universe with God. He chose to live on the Earth for about 33 years before sacrificing His human life for the redemption of our sins. Jesus was the perfect Lamb of God sacrifice to provide salvation for all who repent and accept His grace through faith and baptism.

God created this universe so humans could have an Earthly experience and learn how to transition from a worldly and temporary existence to a spiritual and eternal existence. You will recall that Romans 12:2 advises us to not be conformed to the world, but be transformed in our minds. When we are transformed in our thinking about life and our behavior, we release the old ways and intentionally adopt to God's ways in our thoughts, speech, and actions.

As you know, Biblical scripture is active and alive, (Hebrews 4:12). These divine words represent Godly thoughts, which become active and alive in the minds and hearts of those who hear, read, and accept them. As we have discussed, upon baptism the Holy Spirit dwells within us and helps us, guides us, and sometimes intercedes in our prayers to God on our behalf. (Romans 8:26, 27) The Holy Spirit is a friend and mentor. This is a wonderful blessing to have while we are still in these imperfect bodies.

My rudimentary assessment of the key attributes that we humans are equipped with in this universe include the following:

Physical—Body
Spiritual—Soul
Mind—Thoughts
Heart—Emotions

What we choose to do with these human qualities is up to us. While recognizing that our soul, thoughts, and emotions are spiritual, the lusts of the body often dominate us. But we can escape from the confines of our bodies through our thoughts, emotions, and soul. Reading a stimulating book takes us to places never before imagined. Seeing a wonderful painting or listening to beautiful music allows us to slip into a soothing dimension of joy or peace. Meditating on God's Word causes it to grow more clearly in our hearts and minds.

In this amazing universe that God created, we are not confined to our physical limitations. We have minds that can learn whatever we choose to study, imagine, or discover. By thinking and doing righteous things, we can produce the spiritual fruits as described in Galatians 5:22–23, *"love, joy, peace, patience, gentleness, faithfulness, and self-control, against such things is no law."*

These fruits of the spirit are magnificent blessings if we chose to adopt them as personal characteristics by bearing them in life. The Law of Attraction, as some people label it, presumes that we receive what we meditate on or worry about. In this case, a positive attitude is very important, especially when we are challenged in some way. Pray about worrisome things, ask God's help and trust Him.

We have hearts that can open wide and emit immeasurable love for heavenly and earthly beings, and we have spiritual souls that can soar wherever we wish to go. In this grand universe, we have God-given liberty. We can learn to master ourselves by mastering our thoughts to be in concert with His truths. If we have this much ability in this physical universe, we can only imagine how much liberty we will have in God's heavenly universe without fleshly bodies. And remember, Heaven is inundated with love, joy, peace, and praise.

In this next chapter, you will get a synopsis of what the Bible tells us God wants Christians to become and accomplish on this earth. It is a perfect GPS road map for terrestrial and eternal success!

Chapter 6

Our Reasonable Service

Hopefully this primer has you thinking about accepting Jesus as your Savior, rejuvenating your relationship with Him, or enriching your relationship with Him. If so, this beautiful new circumstance produces one additional question. You have read much about what God, Jesus, and the Holy Spirit do for us, but what must we do for them? This is the question that is addressed in this narrative.

Fortunately, we don't have to guess what this involves. We turn to His Word to learn what it says. We have already reviewed God's two great commandments to love God and love others, (Matthew 22:37–39). God's great commission to all Christians is to go into the world spreading the gospel of Christ and baptizing them, (Matthew 28:29–30).

The law of "*cause* and *effect*" and its corollaries of "we reap what we sow," or the "principle of reciprocity" are always at work. God loves us and we are returning our love for him. Our love for others draws the love of others to us. And we are happy to spread the good news (gospel) about Jesus and His saving grace because of what we know He can do for them, now and eternally!

God does not expect us to be perfect even after we are baptized into Jesus. We needed Jesus to wash away our sins at baptism and we need Him to continue doing so when we inevitably transgress. As Christians, God hears our prayers for forgiveness and redemption throughout this life. As a member of the kingdom of Christ, God always supports us, as does Jesus, the Holy Spirit, angels, and fellow Christians. Of course, we are expected to continue learning about and emulating Jesus, by obeying God's Commands, following the Holy Spirit's spiritual guidance, and worshiping with fellow Christians.

In 1 Corinthians 13:12–13, we are told that while on Earth, we see in a mirror dimly, but now we must abide faith, hope, and love and the greatest of these is love. But we are not alone. As you know, the Holy Spirit dwells within all Christians. The highly appreciated evangelist and author, Charles Stanley wrote a seminal book titled, *The Spirit-Filled Life* in which he encourages us to discover the joy of surrendering to the Holy Spirit and lists some of God's principles for Christian living. (244)

1. We always reap what we sow, (Galatians 6:7).
2. The people with whom we spend time will influence the direction of our lives, (Proverbs 13:20).
3. The person who hates to be corrected will eventually make stupid mistakes, (Proverbs 12:10).

Some additional Biblical principles for Christian living that I find very useful are listed:

- In Ephesians 6:5–8 we are told to serve God, not man.
- In Luke 9:62 we are told not to look back, but go forward in Christ.
- In Hebrews 10:23–25 we are told to hold fast to our hope, encouraging one another.
- In Hebrews 12:2 we learn to fix our eyes on Jesus.
- In Romans 5:1 we learn to be faithful to God.
- In 1 Corinthians 16:14 we learn to do all things in love.
- In Matthew 5:16 we learn to let our lights shine to glorify our Father.
- Jeremiah 29:13 says when we seek God, we will find Him if we seek him with all our heart.
- In Proverbs 3:5–6 we are told, *"Trust in the Lord with all your heart, and do not lean on your own understanding. In all your ways acknowledge Him, and He will make your paths straight."*

In summary, Christians are asked to love God, Jesus, and the Holy Spirit, surrender to Jesus, love and serve others, spread the Gospel, do good works, and remain faithful.

Jason Moon, another respected preacher, advises Christians to, "Preach or teach the Gospel; use words if necessary." In other words, walk the walk and set the worthy example of being a Child of God.

Some of you may be thinking, "What are God's rewards for our Godly service?" It is an interesting question. We already know that we are loved. We would not even be here to ask questions except for our loving God who created us. The entire universe and God's plan is for us to have the opportunity to live with him by accepting His son and serving His cause to seek and save the lost. Remember, all humans are sinners in the flesh, but God does not want any to be lost. (2 Peter 3:9) His saving grace is a given to those who make the **ultimate choice** to accept it. In John 10:10, we learn that Jesus gives His people more abundant life, and 1 Peter 1:3–4 says God has saved us and we have an inheritance that is imperishable, reserved for us in heaven.

Can we out give God? By no means. Everything has been created by Him, but He wants a personal relationship with each of us. He is our heavenly Father and we know that fathers, like mothers, want to know, love, teach, and nurture their children. He has given us life on this fallen world and sacrificed His only heavenly Son to atone for our sins that we might someday also live with Him in heaven. It appears that loving and praising God, His Son, and the Holy Spirit is truly a reasonable service! Romans 12:1 reads, *"I beseech you therefore, brethren, by the mercies of God, that ye present your bodies a living sacrifice, holy, acceptable unto God, which is your reasonable service."* (KJV)

Prayer

Prayer is a supernatural gift. As we conclude, this is a good time to reinforce the gift of prayer since it is the way we communicate and build relationships with God, Jesus, and the Holy Spirit through our short time in this world.

Many books and sermons have been based on this incredible communication device between us and deity. My goal here is not to provide a dissertation on the subject, but to remind readers that prayer is a personal way to communicate with our Father. In Matthew 6:6, Jesus tells the disciples to pray in their secret closets unlike the Pharisees who prayed loudly in public to bring attention to themselves. And don't worry about whether God hears you, because He knows our needs before we even bring them to His attention. But He still yearns to hear from us.

Matthew 21:22 and Mark 11:24 tell us to pray *believing* what we ask for. In the book of James 5:15, we are told to pray for others who are suffering or sick and to pray with *faith*. Not all prayers include requests of our Father. He also wants our praise and thanks for his love, guidance, protection, and answered prayers.

Please be reminded that God will grant whatever is in His will and in His time because He is omniscient, knowing all things and what is best for us at the time. 1 John 5:14 says, *"And this is the confidence that we have before Him, that, if we ask anything according to His will, He hears us."*

Prayer is also the perfect venue to confess and repent our sins and ask for His strength so we can resist those temptations in the future. In prayer, we can and must be completely truthful, humble, and candid as possible in the same way we want our children to be honest with us.

In Colossians 4:2 we are told to be devoted to prayer and be thankful. In first Thessalonians 5:16–18 we are told to rejoice and pray without ceasing.

Jesus gave His disciples clear instructions in Matthew 6–7 about prayer and they are still applicable to us in this time.

Do we always need to verbalize our prayers? No. God knows what we are thinking and He knows what is in our hearts.

Do we always have to pray with our eyes closed? Not when you are driving your automobile!

Do we always have to pray in the name of Jesus? Absolutely! In several places in the New Testament, including John 16:23, we are told to pray to God in the name of Jesus.

I have an important point to mention about prayer. There are times when prayers are unanswered. Usually it appears to be because God knows what's best for us in the long run, and we don't. At other times, it appears that the request is within His will, but the timing is bad for some reason known only by God. Sometimes, however, we need to remember that people have free will to think and act. For example, we all pray for good health and safety for our loved ones. But if they abuse their bodies with an unhealthy lifestyle (cause), they will likely suffer unhealthy consequences (effect). If they choose to drive their autos recklessly (cause), they will likely crash (effect). In these circumstances, we should not blame God.

God follows His laws of the universe which He set fast for everyone. However, He is a merciful God and is concerned about His children when they mourn. Like the father in the parable of the prodigal son, God waits patiently for them to come to Him for consolation.

The Bible provides a great example of His sympathy for us. Psalm 34:18 says, *"The Lord is near to the brokenhearted, and saves those who are crushed in spirit."* Prayer is a wonderful gift and it helps us build an intimate relationship with deity which produces peace, joy, faith, and comfort.

I can't wait for you to read this last chapter. In it you will get a peek at the nature of God by examining his wisdom and will as revealed in the scriptures. We have two infallible examples to follow as we grow spiritually. These perfect examples are God and His Son Jesus. Fasten your seatbelt, you are in for an illuminating experience!

Chapter 7
Seek Wisdom Not Gold

W e live in a multi-dimensional existence whether we recognize it or not. We know that we live in a fallen world and the ruler of this world is Satan, (1 John 5:19). We also know that Jesus came to seek and save the lost and defeat the Devil. Jesus achieved both goals by dying on the cross, being resurrected, and establishing His kingdom, the church, on Earth. We Christians also know that we have a more powerful spirit within us (Holy Spirit) than he who is in the world, (1 John 4:4). Biblical knowledge is the source of wisdom beyond this world because it comes from God almighty. In Matthew, 6:33, Jesus advised his audience during the Sermon on the Mount, *"But seek first His kingdom and His righteousness and all these things shall be added to you."*

We know that we live in a physical world, but heaven is a spiritual world. We also know that we humans have bodies, souls, minds, and emotions, all of which contribute to the perceptions of ourselves, others, the world, and heaven. It should be no surprise that navigating through all these influences and experiences of life on Earth can be *confusing, exasperating, frightening, and exhausting.* This life can also be *joyful, enlightening, exhilarating, and tranquil.* The first list of adjectives is from the world and the evil one and the second list is from God. We can better participate in the brighter side of life if we first learn about the wisdom of God.

Will bad things happen to Christians? Yes. But we have a host of heavenly personalities that aid and minister to us; God, Jesus, the Holy Spirit, righteous angels. We also have support from fellow Christians, family and friends. As you are aware, in Romans 8:28 we can find comfort when things don't go well because we know that God causes all things to work together for good for Christians.

Will good things happen to Christians? Yes. Christians are part of God's kingdom and we have the only Savior in the universe who is also judge and advocate for all people. We humans cannot fathom all the blessings we are given in this life and the next.

From the Bible we learn that there are two kinds of wisdom, worldly and spiritual. Worldly wisdom is not godly wisdom, (Ephesians 5:8–17, James 4:1–4, and James 3:13–18). Humans cannot obtain perfect ethical wisdom without seeking and acknowledging the Lord in all things. Only then will He direct our paths to His wisdom, (Proverbs 3:5–6). Trying to be just a good person in this world without Jesus misses the goals of serving Christ, having a clear conscience, receiving His salvation and glorifying God.

In John 15:4–5, Jesus says He is the vine and we are the branches. We can do nothing without Him. There are people in this world who believe they alone know how they should live their lives. God also tells us in 1 Corinthians 1:20 that God has made foolish the wisdom of the world.

This intriguing topic of wisdom is spread throughout the Bible, but is given special emphasis in the Books of Psalms, Proverbs, Job, and Ecclesiastes. I highly recommend you study the scriptures in these precious books. Don't read them to identify your purpose for the rest of your life. Rather, read them to identify God's purpose for the rest of your life.

We can learn about God's wisdom through the Bible, but if we don't understand it or practice it, it is useless. A rising South Carolina preacher, Keaton Pearce says, "Knowledge by its self is of little benefit if you don't put it to good use." He is correct, of course. We can learn about God's wisdom by seeking wisdom scriptures, reading parables, and especially reading the red letters in most Bibles that indicate words spoken by Jesus. We can also learn God's wisdom from Christian preachers and Christian books. But the most important thing is to practice discerning the difference between good and evil, truth and untruth.

I once heard the comment that wisdom is evidence that a person has learned to govern themselves. This is a good definition, but Webster's Dictionary is more descriptive, "Wisdom is more than just knowledge, intelligence, or practicality. It's a type of accumulated knowledge that's usually applied with a sense of empathy, ethics, and enlightenment." Keaton Pearce once provided this insight relevant to this discussion, "Embracing His wisdom and aligning ourselves with His righteousness brings clarity, integrity, and a sense of purpose to our lives."

The Bible describes wisdom as being more valuable than gold and jewels, (Proverbs 16:16; 8:11). Wisdom gives blessings and keeps us from evil, (Proverbs 3:13; 5:1–6). We can also depend on Godly wisdom to bear many blessings, (James 3:13–17). This series of verses begins: *"Who among you is wise and understanding? Let him show by his good behavior his deeds in the gentleness of wisdom."*

The Bible also tells us that the Wisdom of God is *universal,* (Daniel 2:20–22), *infinite,* (Psalm 147:5), *inscrutable,* (Isaiah 40:28), *mighty,* (Job 36:5), and *perfect,* (Job 37:16).

We Christians have the wonderful gift of Godly wisdom to learn about and replicate in our Earthly lives. James 1:5–6 advises that in prayer we should ask God for wisdom, and it will be given to us if we ask in faith. The benefits to us, and those with whom we interact, are highly improved when we pray for and accept His wisdom. We should habitually listen closely and ask more questions to focus on the needs of others as we strive to put His wisdom to use.

Solomon, the son of King David, was asked by God what he wanted from God as he assumed the throne. In 1 Kings 3:9 Solomon replied, *"So Give Thy servant an understanding heart to judge Thy people, to discern between good and evil."* God found great favor in Solomon's answer and made him the wisest man in the world. It is my prayer that we all may learn to discern good from evil just like Solomon. If we do this, we will find favor from God. Remember always the words of the Apostle Paul in 1 Corinthians 2:5, *"And your faith should not rest on the wisdom of men, but on the power of God."* Remember also that by God's calling, we are in Christ Jesus, who became to us wisdom, righteousness, sanctification and redemption, (1 Corinthians 1:30).

I will leave you with this final piece of Biblical wisdom when Joshua admonished his fellow Israelites to make a decision for God, Joshua 24:17, *"...choose for yourselves today whom you will serve, ...but as for me and my house, we will serve the Lord."*

Thank you for reading this primer of His divine word. It is my prayer that each of you have made the **ultimate choice** to serve Jesus, be restored with Him, or have decided to get more involved in His cause. Your reward will be to live with Him happily ever after.

Post Notes

If you have made a positive choice in your mind or if you are still thinking about it, I encourage you to accept the Lord and His word by attending a Bible-based, baptizing church. Read the Bible for yourself. If possible, get mentored with a Christian who believes the whole Bible or join a serious Bible study group that studies the Bible only.

For your convenience, I am repeating the Biblically-based succession for embracing baptism and be listed in the Lamb's Book of Life.

1. *Hear* (learn) about Jesus, our savior, Romans 10:14.
2. *Believe* Jesus is our savior; there are no others, John 14:6.
3. *Repent* of our sins knowing that *"all have sinned and fall short of the Lord,"* Romans 3:23, and *"The wages of sin is* death but *the free gift of God is eternal life in Christ Jesus our Lord,"* Romans 6:23.
4. *Confess* our belief that Jesus is the Son of God and our Savior, Romans 10:10.

5. Be *baptized* with immersion as Jesus demonstrated, John 3:1–5, Acts 2:38, and Acts 8:34–39.
6. Stay *faithful* to your conversion for the rest of you life, 2 Timothy 3:14–15.

I also recommend visiting the most supernatural museum in our nation's Capital. The Museum of the Bible, the first and only of its kind. It is a stimulating and enlightening experience.

When you discover the comfort that memorizing scripture provides, you will become a lifelong advocate of this rewarding habit. I hope you will start with the only verse we carved into the Jerusalem stone entrance wall at Museum of the Bible in Washington. Not surprisingly, it is a *cause* and *effect* sentence, *"Thy word is a lamp unto my feet, and a light unto my path."* (Psalm 119:105).

Finally, no matter what circumstances you encounter during this life, always remember Jesus's invitation to all Christians, *"Behold, I stand at the door and knock; if anyone hears my voice and opens the door, I will come in to him, and will dine with him, and he with me."* (Revelation 3:20)
May God continue to bless you, everyone.

References

Allen, James. *As A Man Thinketh*. Collins Publishing, London.

Bonhoeffer, Dietrich, Newstimes.com, December, 2024.

Green, Steve & Hillard, Todd. *The Bible in America*. Dust Jacket Press, 2013.

Hurt, John M. *A Bookmark of Basic Bible References*. Hurt Publications, Smyrna, Tennessee.

McDowell, Josh & McDowell, Sean. *Evidence That Demands a Verdict*. 2nd Edition, Thomas Nelson Publishing, 2017.

New American Standard Bible—The Open Bible Edition. Thomas Nelson Publishers, 1977.

NewsTimes.org, December 2024. Bonhoeffer's letter to Schleicher.

Ortberg, John. *The Life You've Always Wanted*. Zondervan Publishing House, 1997.

Ross, Hugh. "Reason to Believe" online article extracted from his book, *Fulfilled Prophecy: Evidence for the Reality of the Bible*. Apologetics articles for "Reason to Believe Ministry." 2003–24.

Shank, Michael. *Muscle and a Shovel*. Shank Ministries, 2011.

Stanley, Charles F. *The Spirit-Filled Life*. Thomas Nelson Publishing, 2014.

Webster, Allen. *You Can't Get to Heaven Alone. www.gladtidingspublishing. com*

Webster's Dictionary. *Merriam-webster.com*

Wycliffe Global Alliance Statistics. *Wycliffe.net*

www.ingramcontent.com/pod-product-compliance
Lightning Source LLC
LaVergne TN
LVHW010318070426
835508LV00033B/3499